Financial Freedom Too

Surviving the Layoff-Era

Volume 2

Seek Financial Freedom Too

By

Keith Outerbridge

DEDICATION

To My 2 Boys <u>Reese</u> and <u>Ruben</u>

As you grow older in life may you survive and be entrepreneurs in life.

Use your mind to create jobs, opportunities and businesses for you and

Future generations to come.

Remember, Daddy Always Love you

Table of Contents

INTRODUCTION

I remember when I was 21 years old working for a small brokerage firm on Wall Street. The year was 1989.

The boss told all the traders to go to lunch and be back at the office for a 2:00 pm meeting. A long lunch break many thought, but a much needed time for a "stressful" securities trader.

Once back at the office. All of our belongings were in a box with our names on it.

The boss said "Due to the economic decline in our business, your services are no longer needed". We all faced a new dilemma,

"LAY-OFFS". And we thought times were good in the late 80's.

* Many of my co-workers, who worked at the brokerage firm for 15 years or more began "crying".

* Many were angry at how they told us.

* Some were upset that they displaced us into the unemployment line.

Me.... I was young, so I thought I will find another job elsewhere and I did.

In the early 90's, you could quit a job and find another before the weekend.

Now in the year 2012. You Can't. Jobs are few and Skills are necessary.

In 1992, I had written a book called **"Financial Freedom:** *A Special Guide to Understanding Investing."*

20 years later what I had to say in that book held true and has remained true unless you **change financially** and "**seize the opportunity**".

We all want to seek Financial Freedom Too. But when faced with a job loss, you must seek Freedom Too.

This is a survival guide to surviving Lay-offs, during a recession.

Hopefully, this book will inspire you, allow you to think and re-think positive, while you are experiencing the layoff period.

So seek Financial Freedom Too. It's the only choice you have!!!!!

Foreword

You have just been lay-off, downsized and re-organized at work. You are now officially unemployed...What do you do? Cry, get angry or get yourself together and go back out there.

If you choose the later, Financial Freedom too will become within reach.

So what plan do you have when the Boss tells you?
"Your Job is no longer available", you are being "Let Go", "Downsized", Re-Organized", "Unemployed", "Fired",

Surviving the layoff era:

First, you must start out with a **plan**. Gather yourself and thoughts.

This book will help you sought out a **plan** that is right for you.

In this book you will *learn how to have a plan, execute it by putting it into action.* Understand that you are not alone and many will go through this process as well. Use this book to guide yourself through the unemployment process and what to look for, do and plan for future layoffs.

Start with a **PLAN**

Here are some ideas to start with,

Plan A: start collecting bottles for money

Plan B: go to websites to become a tester.

* They pay you to test products

Plan C: Think of a small business to start, cleaning, janitorial or service rendered.

Look for recession proof jobs, Fast food, quick service jobs.

Then franchise it out.

Plan D: Go back to School and Learn Something New.

 A Trade

Plan E: Where to go to Make Money?

Plan F: What to do with Made Money?

Purchase **Financial Freedom ONE: A Special Guide to Investing**

A Must have book.

Plan G: Where to Spend Money?

Plan H: Watch the Market Trends. Don't invest in it yet.

Plan I: What to Invest in a Recession?

These are just some of the examples and ideas to get your mind off being unemployed. Continue reading and you will find more.......

This book will focus on the following chapters

Chapter 1: Recession Proof Jobs to get

Chapter 2: Recession Proof Business to Invest in

Chapter 3: Planning for Future Lay-Offs: Get an Education. Go back and learn something new. Revamp your Resume

Chapter 4: How to get a dollar?

Chapter 5: How to Save a Dollar?

Chapter 6: How to Spend a Dollar Wisely?

Chapter 7: Market Trends in a Recession?

Chapter 8: How to Invest That Dollar in a Recession?

Table of Contents

Chapter 1: Recession Proof Jobs

In an industry of jobs available, there are some jobs that are recession proof. Free from Recession because no matter what the economy does we need them. Such as Doctors, for when you get sick someone must be there to care for you. Farmers who grow food so we can all eat. Car mechanics and people who troubleshoot and support electronic devices. These are all highly skilled jobs that are recession free.

They are in demand and are needed no matter how bad the economy is financially in the world.

10 Recession-Proof Jobs
Rachel Zupek, CareerBuilder.com writer

It's safe to say that the current job market is in the pits.

Since the recession began in December 2007, 4.4 million jobs have been lost; more than half of that decline occurred between November 2008 and February 2009, according to the most recent data from the Bureau of Labor Statistics.* Additionally, there are 12.5 million unemployed people and the unemployment rate was 8.1 percent in February 2009. Also in that month, employment declined in nearly all major industries.

The only industry to add jobs in February was health care, with a gain of 27,000 jobs. Job growth occurred in ambulatory health care and in hospitals, adding 16,000 and 7,000 jobs, respectively, according to the BLS.

While there doesn't seem to be much certainty about the economy, there is one fact that remains true no matter what: Certain industries are recession-resistant.

"Some jobs are recession-proof because they provide goods or services that are essential to everyday life," says Laurence Shatkin, Ph.D., author of "150 Best Recession-Proof Jobs." "Other recession-proof jobs protect us from harm and make the justice system work."

For example, Shatkin cites water and liquid waste treatment plant operators as a recession-proof job because "even in the most dire economic times, people need to drink, wash and flush."

While nobody's job is 100 percent secure, plenty of jobs and industries are somewhat resilient. For boosted job security, Shatkin suggests looking for work not only in a recession-resistant occupation, but also within a recession-resistant industry.

For instance, he says that people tend to forget that the education industry employs many people who aren't teachers; health care employs workers who never come near a patient; and the high-tech industry employs many people who aren't engineers or technicians.

If you're looking for a new job, focus your efforts on the following areas and you might increase your odds of landing a great position.

1. Registered nurse   Resistant reason: Nurses are always in demand, recession or not. People will continue to get sick and seek medical attention no matter what the state of the economy, which ought to give RNs sound job security.   **Training needed:** A bachelor's or associate degree in nursing, plus completion of an approved nursing program. RNs must also complete a national licensing examination to obtain a nursing license. Further training or education qualifies nurses to work in specialty areas.   **Growth through 2016*:** 23.5 percent   **Salary**:** $46,242

2. Public relations specialist   Resistant reason: As advertising budgets are sliced and other marketing efforts are nixed to cut costs, many companies will rely solely on their public relations departments to promote the company brand. Additionally, as rumors spread about layoffs, bailouts and bankruptcy, PR specialists are needed more than ever to put out these fires along the way.   **Training needed:** A college degree in a communications-related field like journalism or advertising is helpful, though not necessary. If you lack a degree, employers will look for demonstrated communication skills.   **Growth through 2016:** 18 percent   **Salary:** $41,549

3. Teacher, post-secondary   Resistant reason: Since it's becoming harder to score a job, people are riding out the recession by going back to school. Furthermore, workers and job seekers alike are earning higher education to increase their marketability in the work force.   **Training needed:** Training varies based on the subject you teach and where you teach it. Four-year colleges and universities, however, usually require candidates to hold a doctoral degree for full-time, tenure-track positions.   **Growth through 2016:** 23 percent   **Salary:** $46,991

4. Police officer   Resistant reason: First, police officers are employed by the government, which definitely doesn't hurt job security. Second, the sad fact is that crime happens every day and the economy isn't helping. Desperate times call for desperate measures, which for some people include stealing and other offenses -- in some areas, police officers are busier than ever.   **Training needed:** Law enforcement agencies encourage applicants to take courses or training related to law enforcement subjects after high school. Candidates must be U.S. citizens, usually at least 20 years old, and must meet rigorous physical and personal qualifications.   **Growth through 2016:** 11 percent   **Salary:** $49,288

5. Insurance sales agent   Resistant reason: Though many Americans are on a tight budget, people are generally willing to spend money on the big stuff, such as coverage for natural disasters, health-care expenses and automobile accidents. With so many people losing their jobs -- leaving them uninsured as a result -- insurance sales agents have a larger client pool to work with.   **Training needed:** You have to have a state license to sell insurance; requirements vary by state, but generally require insurance-related course work and passing several exams. A college degree is not required, but is strongly encouraged.   **Growth through 2016:** 13 percent   **Salary:** $39,656

6. Pharmacy technician   Resistant reason: As the population ages, people probably will need more medication, as do the many people suffering from depression and anxiety as a result of the recession. Plus, many people have health-care coverage of some kind, even with the downturn, which makes it possible for people to continue to pay for medications. **Training needed:** Most are trained on the job, but employers prefer applicants who have formal training, certification or previous experience. **Growth through 2016:** 32 percent **Salary:** $28,624

7. Funeral director **Resistant reason:** Death is a fact of life. No matter what the economy does, people will continue to pass away and families will continue to grieve while seeking assistance to plan services for their loved ones. **Training needed:** Every state requires that funeral directors are licensed. State licensing laws vary, but most require you to be 21 years old, have two years of formal education, serve a one-year apprenticeship and pass an examination. **Growth through 2016:** 12 percent **Salary:** $87,383

8. Environmental science technician **Resistant reason:** The Obama administration plans to create 5 million "green" jobs over the next 10 years. Despite a slowing economy, a large percentage of the U.S. work force continues to dedicate itself to the environment. **Training needed:** Most environmental science technicians need an associate degree or certificate in applied science or science-related technology. Technicians with a high school diploma and no college degree typically begin work under the direct supervision of an experienced technician and eventually earn a two-year degree in science technology. **Growth through 2016:** 28 percent **Salary:** $36,655

9. Network systems and data communications analyst **Resistant reason:** Many technology-based positions can be performed by outsourcing, but certain technology workers, such as network systems and data communications analysts, must deal with problems onsite. **Training needed:** An associate degree or certificate is sufficient; although more advanced positions might require a computer-related bachelor's degree. **Growth through 2016:** 53.4 percent **Salary:** $40,827 and $71,637, respectively

10. Fast-food worker **Resistant reason:** Unfortunately, fast food is all some people can afford these days. While so many other companies saw a decrease in sales and income last year, McDonalds, for example, saw global sales increase 6.9 percent throughout 2008, and its operational income increased 14 percent. **Training needed:** No previous training is needed for this position; on-the-job training is provided. **Growth through 2016:** 17 percent **Salary:** $16,568.

Recession Proof Job Sectors

- **Health Care:** People will always get sick — sometimes even more so when they don't have the insurance or money to take preventative measures or eat healthy food.
- **Energy:** Although consumers are likely to cut back, they're not going to stop using energy. In fact, this industry may grow, as companies look for more efficient ways to deliver using less energy.
- **Education:** No matter how dire the economy is, there are always jobs for teachers. Kids will still go to school, and many out-of-work adults may decide to continue their education.
- **Utilities:** Just like the energy sector, it's safe to assume that people are not going to stop lighting their homes. So utility administration, maintenance and other related jobs should remain intact.
- **International Business:** Even when the economy is doing poorly in the U.S., other countries may be doing well. So if you are involved in international business, you can expect your career to stay safe.
- **Public Safety:** Police layoffs are very rare, especially at a time where public safety is threatened by desperate criminals. A career in public safety is almost guaranteed to be secure.
- **Funerals**: Just like people won't stop getting sick, they'll continue to die as well, so as morbid as it is, morticians will always have customers.
- **Accounting:** Death and taxes are a sure thing. In a recession, people and companies are likely to get desperate for more deductions and a hard look at their books.
- **Federal Government:** Most federal-government jobs end only when workers retire. Additionally, government services tend to step up in times of recession, so your chances of getting and keeping a government job are good.
- **Pharmaceuticals:** As long as doctors prescribe them, people are still going to take drugs. So whether you're behind the pharmacy counter or in the lab, you can rest easy.
- Sales: As a general rule, anyone who is a source of income for a company will be

safe, so salespeople — especially in recession-proof industries — have little to worry about.

- **Military:** The military is always hiring, especially during wartime. Also, consider that most of your living expenses are covered, so cost-of-living expenses are not really a concern.
- **Gambling:** When times get tough, people seek an outlet. One of those outlets is gambling, especially because it offers a chance to turn financial troubles around.
- **Alcohol:** Alcohol is another outlet for troubled times, so distributors and manufacturers in this industry will continue to thrive.
- **Politics:** Even in a recession, public officials are still around earning tidy sums, which are often tied to the cost of living.
- **Skilled Services:** Hair will always grow, and drains will always clog, so you can expect steady work in skilled services like plumbing and hairstyling.
- **Debt Management:** Recessions mean crunch time for debtors, and they're sure to need some guidance.
- **Consulting:** Recessions are crunch times for companies as well, and they're likely to bring in consultants for advice on efficiency and squeezing the most out of their resources.
- **Bankruptcy Law:** It's sad, but true: As companies and individuals go bankrupt, they'll need a lawyer to help them work through it all.
- **Government Contracting:** Despite money troubles, roads must be maintained and schools must be built. Contract your work out for government functions for job security.
- **Food:** People need food to survive, and it's not likely that anyone is going to just stop eating — no matter how bad the economy gets.
- **Beauty, Health and Erotic Services**: Regardless of a recession, people who enjoy being pampered will seldom give up the simple pleasures in life.
- **Debt Collection:** As budgets get squeezed, people will fall behind on payments, and companies will look to debt collectors to recoup their costs.
- **Ultraluxury Items:** If you're in a business that caters to the ultrarich, you can expect to be safe, as this type of consumer is likely to have measures in place to weather the recession.
- **Multifaceted Careers:** If you don't put all of your eggs in one basket, you should be able to ride out a recession by relying on secondary income. So if you juggle a career that involves a regular job, plus other sources like online income, <u>freelancing</u> and investing, numerous failures have to happen before you're really in trouble.

Although today's job market may be bleak, there are some bright spots if you know where to look. While recessions hit some sectors hard, others go on like clockwork — or even experience growth. So whether you're hunting for a job or still feeling ostensibly secure now is a good time to evaluate your options and consider one of the aforementioned recession-proof careers.

If all of the above jobs do not work…

Then you need to seek Financial Freedom Too.

- Build Wealth - Invest
- Create your own job - Create a Successful Business.

When you own your own business, you no longer have to worry about laying-off yourself. The Boss and owner will be you.

Seize the Opportunity and Seek Financial Freedom Too.

Jobs Losses from 2007-2010

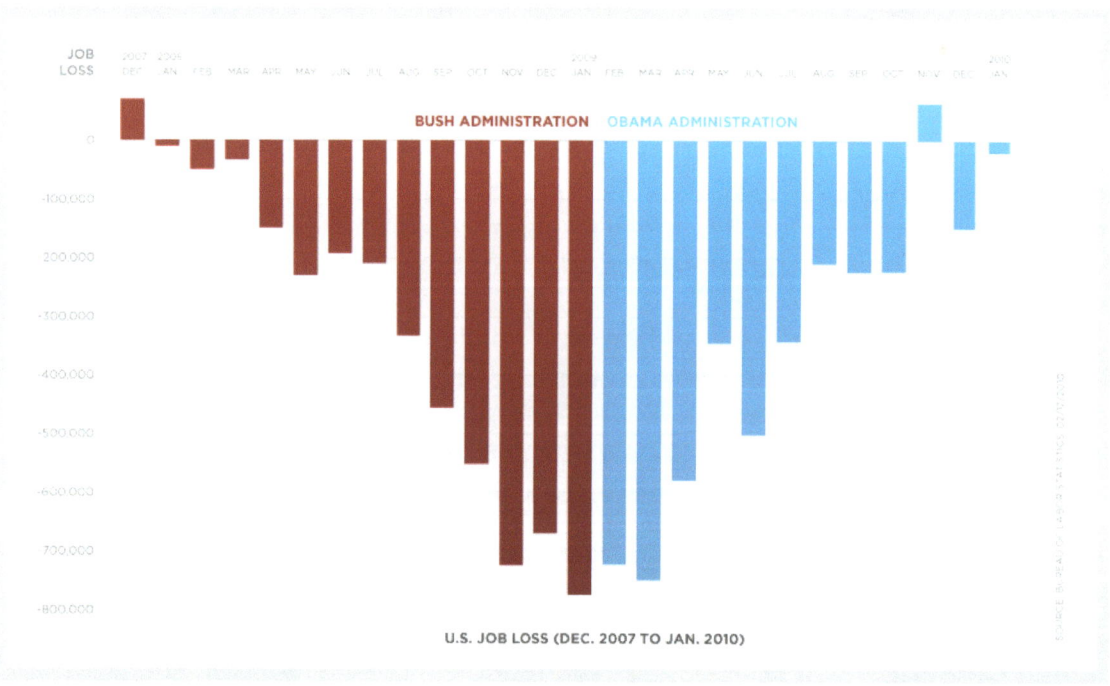

U.S. JOB LOSS (DEC. 2007 TO JAN. 2010)

The unemployment rate has been stagnant at 9.1%. Americans are either looking for work or worried about losing their jobs.

People rally for jobs at the federal courthouse Oct. 13, 2011, in Las Vegas. Nevada's unemployment rate is highest in the nation.

While there's no guarantee against a layoff, there are ways to assess your job security, labor experts say.

"You really need to understand your company's current and evolving strategy. Get as much information as you can," says Ron Brown, a San Francisco-based management consultant who has worked with Fortune 100 companies.

In fact, with so much anxiety surrounding jobs and the economy, more Americans are taking severe steps to prevent a layoff. They're working 70-hour weeks and risking their health and quality of life to keep so-called extreme jobs, according to the Center for Work-Life Policy in New York City.

Understanding Your Risks

One of the key steps to protecting yourself from a potential layoff is awareness — more specifically, avoiding denial. Daniel Hamermesh, an economics professor at the University of Texas at Austin, has studied how workers behave in factories that experienced downturns. Despite signs of slowing business, workers still were surprised when plants finally closed. "Workers are not good in predicting this," says Hamermesh.

That's because workers generally lay low as a job-security defense mechanism, explains management consultant Brown. "People put their heads down and hope for the best, and that's not the best strategy to take," he says.

Instead, Brown advises a game plan that includes assessing the vulnerability of your company and position. That means understanding the evolving business strategy, and how your unit and your specific function fit into the company's overall scheme.

Brown says questions to ask yourself include: Where does your business unit fit into that strategy? Could your unit get spun off or reduced?

Another tip — look at your job function and team from a budgetary point of view. Is the money for your department trending up or down?

While Brown cautions against asking your boss directly about your job's future, there's nothing threatening about talking generally about how business is faring. Sources of information can include supervisors, colleagues, and outside vendors and suppliers.

"You're looking for all indicators that would tell you the strength of your position, or the weakness of your position," says Brown. Based on the information you gather, your options may include pitching yourself to another business unit with a position that matches your skill set.

Ultimately, all signs may point to sending out your resume. It's all about hedging your options in this economy, he says.

More Unemployed 'Long-Termers'

Unemployment is likely to notch higher, to 9.5% in the near term, according to the UCLA Anderson Forecast's September report.

"Even by the end of 2013 we will not be back to the unemployment levels of late 2007," according to the forecast's senior economist David Shulman.

Many workers have returned to school, retired, or stayed home to raise children. Others have left the workforce and given up looking for work.

Indeed, long-term unemployment, defined by those out of work at least 27 weeks or more than two years, has risen higher following the 2007-09 recession than after any other recent recession, according to economist Sylvia Allegretto of the Institute for Research on Labor and Employment at the University of California, Berkeley. Roughly 42% of unemployed Americans are "long-termers."

That's why Brown argues even if you do get laid off, time and energy spent collecting information about your company and your industry will be valuable in a job search.

"The relationships you developed while you gathered this information, these will be critical relationships to move on to your next opportunity," says Brown.

Leverage online job resources.

This one is pretty obvious…. I've found many jobs online — either by contacting recruiters in my area or by making inquiries at particular job boards and job sites. Depending on the type of work you do, certain sites may work out better for you than others, as far as generating job leads. Some well rated sites include:

- **Monster.com**: ranks in the top 20 of most visited web sites in existence. It's recognized as one of the most popular job search engines in the world. It's also the largest, as it houses job postings and resumes numbering in the millions.
- **Job.com**: a resource for local jobs, career advice and other services to manage your job and career.

- **Executive Search Online**: a leading nationwide job matching service for more experienced executives. Pay levels for these executive jobs are typically higher.
- **Beyond.com**: an extensive career network that's set up as a community of niche sites in various industries.
- **EssayEdge**: an essay editing resource for those who need a little help

with their college, graduate or other academic admission essays. They help out students seeking to gain admission to the colleges and universities of their choice.

- **ResumeEdge**: a resume editing resource for those who need a little help writing a high quality resume and / or cover letter. They are the leading provider of resume writing services online and the chosen resume partner of well-known job sites such as Yahoo! Hot Jobs, CareerJournal and Dice.com.
- **Resume Rabbit**: a resume distribution service that submits your resume to top online job banks such as Monster, HotJobs, Career Builder, Dice, etc, as well as job search engines.
- **Snag A Job**: a tool to help you find hourly jobs. This job site specializes in finding part-time and full-time hourly jobs.
- **Yahoo Hot Jobs**: a popular online job board.

The best way to use job sites is to use them to give you leads on potential jobs. You may have to do some filtering and research to sidestep the bogus jobs that may be listed on these places.

6. Conserve your emergency fund?

Hopefully you've been able to stash enough cash in your emergency fund to last you through a downturn. Typically it's been recommended that you have at least 6 months' worth of expenses to tide you over. But these days, liquidity is king! If you want to be absolutely certain that your expenses are fully covered if you DO get laid off, then you'll have to rethink how much cash you should hold. Where to put this money? Somewhere ultra safe, such as a **high yield savings account**.

7. Diversify.

Diversification is not just for investments. It also pertains to income generation and wherever else you may be spending your time. If you've got other ways of making money other than through your job, you'll be in much better shape when a recession hits. So if you've got talents and skills, or that **perfect hobby** you can parlay into a business, **you may think about leveraging these things into money making ventures and alternative income streams.**

8. Seek support.

Some people may feel uncomfortable sharing their job loss with their families. Ever hear of those laid off folks who continue the charade of getting up to "go to work", hiding the fact that they've lost their jobs to their families? Well, if instead you decide to seek out support and share your predicament with others, the better your chances of finding a replacement job, as others may pitch in to help you with your search. Plus, it usually feels better (at least it is for me) when people are commiserating with you over your situation.

9. Don't give up.

Don't feel discouraged! It's easy to feel out of sorts when the job search takes longer than you expect. But these days, a lot of people are in the same boat. It's important to stay persistent though and to keep your spirits up when you're on your hunt. Tomorrow may just be the day you land something.

10. Think outside the box.

I've known some people who feel that because they've fulfilled a certain job or role for many years, or because it's always been their ambition to pursue a particular career, that they must, at all costs, continue down a particular path. **But tough times require flexibility, resourcefulness and practical thinking.** I believe that we shouldn't pigeonhole ourselves into specific roles or types of work — go where the demand is (if your skills are a fit), in order to increase your chances of finding work.

Chapter 2: Recession Proof Business to Invest in

Service businesses such as Cleaning, Food, or Support fixes, Car Mechanic, Plumber, Electricians, Computers, and Air Conditioning & Heating etc., provide a low cost - high profit margin.

These businesses are very good during the recession era:

Vending Machine

Candy Machines, Laundromats, Juice Bars

It's an all cash business.

Vending Machines

- **Bulk Gumball & Candy Vending Machines**
- **Coffee Vending Machine**
- **Cold & Frozen Food Vending Machines**
- **Combination Soda/Snack Vending Machines**
- **Custom Vending Machines**
- **Snack Vending Machines**
- **Soda / Soda Drink Vending Machines**

Vending.com offers a full range of vending machines to meet all your vending needs. We provide customers world wide with a quality state of art full service vending experience. We have the largest selection of automatic merchandisers including snack vending machines, cold soda-drink vendors, hot coffee machines, cold and frozen food vending equipment, bulk gumball & candy vending machines and many more. Our full line vending catalog is customizable with your company logo & color scheme.

Call 1-866-657-7549 today to find out how vending services are not only easy to get started, but finance as well. Satisfy your customers every time with reliable vending machines from Vending.com.

Laundromats

- BusinessesForSale.com
- GlobalBX.com
- LoopNet.com (search for the keyword "Laundromat")
- Craigslist.org (for your city look in the business for sale category)
- BusinessNation.com
- BusinessBroker.net
- BizBuySell.com
- PWS Laundry Company's List of Laundromats for Sale

How Much Cash Do I Need to Buy a Laundromat?

August 1, 2011

When people consider buying or building a coin laundry business, one of the first questions they ask is how much money they will need. This is a good question and the answer depends on some important factors discussed below.

Purchase Price

The first factor in determining how much money an investor needs to buy a laundromat is the value of the store. Laundromats typically trade at about 3 to 5 times annual earnings. Keep in mind this is a very rough estimate.

Financing

The second factor in calculating an investor's out-of-pocket cash needed to purchase a laundromat is the amount of financing available. Financing a laundromat purchase usually comes from one of these four sources: a bank, the seller, a hard money lender, friends and family. It is not uncommon to be able to borrow around 60% to 80% of the purchase price.

Improvements and Repairs

Often someone is selling their store because they are retiring and don't want to manage it any more. Another common scenario is that the store needs significant repairs or improvements like all new machines. An experienced business owner with good credit and strong financial statements may even qualify for 100% financing of new equipment depending on the vendor.

Formula

This is the simple formula to determine how much cash you'll need to buy a laundromat business:

Cash needed = Purchase price – Amount financed + Money for immediate repairs or improvements

A Simple Example

Purchase price = $60,000 in annual income x 5 = $300,000
Loan = 70% LTV so $300,000 x .7 = $210,000 (this means $90,000 in down payment)
Repairs & improvement = $20,000 (new signage, repair broken machines, new floor and new paint).

Cash needed = $300,000 – $210,000 + $20,000 = $110,000.

In reality though there are other factors such as a margin of safety and additional borrowing.

- A good owner will have a margin of safety for unanticipated expenses and working capital of $10,000 (minimum) to 10% of the purchase price ($30,000). The additional cash will help cushion uneven revenue flow and stock your change machines, etc.
- The funds needed could come from additional borrowing such as a line of credit or a home equity loan, reducing out-of-pocket cash needed up front but increasing monthly cash flow due to increased debt service.

Thus the true out-of-pocket money needed to buy a laundromat will vary depending on these factors.

Summary

How much money is really needed to buy or start a laundromat business depends on many factors.

A general rule you can apply is assuming that you'll need 1/3 of the purchase price. That would be 1/3 of $300,000 or $100,000 in this example. You can use this as a back-of-the-envelope shortcut. Naturally a safer rule of thumb would be 50% of the purchase price

Juice Bars

Minimum Investment Required: US$60,000 to $80,000

More Information

Fill out the form below and any questions you may have on financing, training, support, available locations, and more will be answered by the most qualified representative from Juice Zone.

Partner with a Global Leader in Food Franchising

26

Juice Zone is an international award winning franchise and a global leader in the booming healthy fast-casual food industry. Our concept is perfectly in tune with the growing demand for healthy, fresh-made foods. Our business is the development of well-designed stores that operate efficiently and profitably, and are located at strategic sites with high foot traffic, visibility and easy access. Our stores offer a fun, upbeat ambience, and feature an exceptional menu of highly nutritious drinks and foods.

Juice Zone's mission is to provide its customers with a fresh and healthy alternative to fast food. We aim to make nutrition delicious, quick and convenient, and to provide every customer with an extraordinary health experience unlike any they've ever tasted!

The Best Menu in the Fast Casual Food Industry

- **Pure Fruit Smoothies** – the healthiest and tastiest in the industry…by far!
- **Freshly Squeezed Juices** – squeezed fresh for optimal health benefits
- **Wraps** – grilled or un-grilled and made fresh to order
- **Paninis** – grilled and made fresh to order
- **Signature Salads** – incredibly fresh
- **Soups** – healthy and wholesome and low-fat
- **Organic Coffee and Herbal Teas**
- Healthy On-The-GO **Snack Food**s

All of menu items are made fresh using only the highest quality ingredients.

Opportunities include Unit, Multi–Unit, Master/Area Development and Co-Branding franchises.

As a turnkey operation, a Juice Zone store is thoroughly invested with the benefits of extensive planning and testing.

Careful consideration of every detail shows in:

- Expert selection of ideal location
- Lease negotiations
- Vibrant design of store's interior and exterior
- Aggressive marketing program with all first class marketing tools
- Highly efficient operations, developed and proven successful
- Comprehensive training, updated each year
- Full spectrum of Juice Zone recipes
- Professional and dedicated on-going support
- Our expertise in supplier relationships, and much more

The Juice Zone franchise advantage shows in every detail of the concept and store operations,

ensuring our commitment to the highest standards, and the success of every franchise. As a leading internationally established brand, Juice Zone has the experienced team, global networks, superior strategy and support systems to help its partners succeed.

Awards
2008: **"Top Food Franchise Trends"** awarded to Juice Zone by Franchise Direct.
2005: **"Top 100 Franchise Brands"** awarded to Juice Zone by European Franchising.
2004: **"Best Business Format for Franchising"** awarded to Juice Zone by Franchise India.

**To find out more about franchise partnership with Juice Zone,
Contact them at http://www.juicezone.com.**

History

Healthy Food, Healthy Growth!

It started with juice.

More accurately, it started with the lack of juice. Chad Parker was running a successful chain of 100 entertainment franchises across Canada when he went in search of a healthy, fresh glass of juice as part of his dedication to living a healthy life style. He discovered there were few choices available. That got Chad to thinking, then acting.

In 1997 he opened his first juice store – the Juice Zone. Customers flooded in, intrigued and grateful for the chance to enjoy a tasty treat that was also good for you. More locations quickly followed. In just three years, Chad realized the amazing potential for his menu of fresh, healthy juice drinks and decided to share the opportunity with others.

He created Fresh & Healthy Brands in order to franchise the Juice Zone concept across Canada and into other countries. The rapid growth of Juice Zone led Chad to develop additional healthy dining concepts, and Yo-Good frozen yogurt soon joined the Fresh & Healthy family, followed closely by Pure

Health with an expanded menu of healthy items. More recently, Go-Grill became the fourth concept under the Fresh & Health Brands umbrella.

Growth and success came quickly. Within just a few years Fresh & Healthy had franchise partners in the United States, Europe and Asia. Today, Fresh & Healthy franchises are in 24 countries. The company's menus of fresh, healthful food and drinks have captured the imagination and taste buds of millions of people who wish to support their healthy life style with nutritious dining.

In addition to providing delicious and healthful meals for customers, Fresh & Healthy Brands is also dedicated to providing the franchise opportunity for individuals seeking a chance to become successful both financially and in their

community.

We invite you to further explore this new franchise opportunity by downloading a free franchise kit. Or contact our franchise director by calling:

1.866.584.2301 (US & Canada)
1.604.918.5076 (Outside US & Canada)

Janitorial Services Franchises

If you're thinking about starting your own business and have only a small amount to invest, you may be considering buying a janitorial services franchise. For a fee, a janitorial service company (the "franchisor") typically provides you (the "franchisee") with customers and marketing, billing and collection services.

Every franchisor has success stories to share. Be cautious. While success in the janitorial service industry is possible, it's not a guarantee.

A glossary of terms commonly used in the franchise industry is included at the end of this brochure.

How Janitorial Services Franchises Work

In a typical janitorial cleaning franchise, you pay the franchisor a fee for a "package" of cleaning accounts. The fee is based on the dollar value of cleaning accounts that the franchisor will make available. The fee usually is about half the gross income the accounts are supposed to generate in a year. For example, for a fee of $10,000, you'll get accounts worth $20,000; for a fee of $15,000, you'll get accounts worth $30,000. You also may have to pay ongoing royalty or management fees.

The franchisor may offer you financing. This may sound especially attractive if you have trouble getting credit from traditional lenders.

The franchisor is supposed to offer you cleaning accounts that will produce the level of income represented in the package you purchased. However, several factors can affect that level of income. For example, if you don't accept an account, the franchisor may not have to offer you a substitute. Or, if you refuse an account because you feel it's located too far away, you may lose your right to that income. Also, if you lose accounts because you did a poor cleaning job, the franchisor doesn't have to replace those accounts.

Problems You May Face

The Federal Trade Commission and the Maryland Attorney General's Office advise you to use caution when thinking about buying a janitorial services franchise, which often appeal to immigrants and others who speak limited English. The franchise agreement you'll receive from the franchisor may be long and complex. It may be difficult to understand your legal rights and obligations, and the obligations of the franchisor. Consider getting professional advice. Ask a lawyer, accountant or business advisor to review the franchise agreement. The money and time you spend on professional help may save you from a bad investment.

Here are some of the problems you may face:

- **Accounts offered versus accounts received.** There may be a difference between the accounts the franchisor promises to offer you and the accounts you actually receive, as well as the revenue that comes with them. For example, the franchisor may promise to offer you accounts generating $1,000 in monthly billings for the first year. To meet its obligations, the franchisor may offer you more than one cleaning account. But given time conflicts, distance issues or other problems, you may not be able to accept all the accounts the franchisor offers. What's more, the franchisor may offer the same accounts to several franchisees on a first-come, first-served basis. If you can't accept an account because you can't get to the location, or if another franchisee accepts the account first, the franchisor may have satisfied its obligation to offer you accounts. Because the franchisor may not tell you about this policy before you buy the "package" of accounts, you should not count on receiving all the revenue that the franchisor promised at first.

- **Rejected accounts.** The franchisor may not have to replace an account that you reject.

- **Franchisor-selected accounts.** The franchisor usually selects accounts for you. The size, number and location of the accounts may not be what you expect. For example, the franchisor may require you to service more than one account at the same time, or the job sites may be far apart.

- **Lost accounts.** Most janitorial franchise agreements specify that if a customer cancels the cleaning contract, the franchisor doesn't have to replace the account for you. In fact, you may have to pay an extra sales and marketing fee for a new account to make up for the lost income.

- **Integration clauses.** The franchise agreement you sign may contain a clause that limits the terms of your agreement to those specifically detailed in the written franchise agreement. This means that any oral claims or promises made by the franchisor are not part of your agreement. This is one reason why it's so important to get all promises in writing in the franchise agreement.

- **First year time lag for receiving accounts.** The package of accounts you buy will suggest a level of income within a year. But the franchisor may take several months to supply you with the promised accounts. That means you may not earn any income until several months after you've purchased the package, so you may not earn the estimated annual income. Therefore, it's important to have other sources of income during your first few months of operation.

- **Ongoing fees.** The franchisor may charge you a monthly management or service fee. You'll have to pay the fee even if you don't have any income from your cleaning business that month. If you finance the franchise fee, you must make the monthly payment on that debt whether or not you're receiving income from the cleaning business. And although you may find customers without the franchisor's help, any income from a cleaning account you solicit will be included when the franchisor calculates the royalty and management fees you owe.

- **Franchisor-owned accounts.** The franchisor may own all the customer accounts, including those that you get on your own. This means that if your franchise agreement ends, you will not be able to service the accounts for which you paid a fee, and you won't be able to service the accounts you got on your own, either.

- **Training.** Get information about the franchisor's training program before you invest. The franchisor decides the type of training you'll get. It may involve watching videos and reading books; it may not involve classroom or on-site training.

- **Contract bidding procedures.** The franchisor may not tell you how it bids for cleaning contracts or what specific services you must provide to the customers. The franchisor may only tell you that you should be able to earn $12 to $15 an hour doing janitorial work. However, when bidding for cleaning contracts, the franchisor may offer your services at a lower rate, and you may have no say in whether the amount charged is reasonable. So even though the account is represented as being worth a certain amount of money, it may not be worth that much to you, and you may not be able to make a profit once you pay for expenses like supplies and transportation costs.

- **Short-term accounts.** People who operate janitorial franchises often find that customers rarely maintain an account for more than a year. That's because customers prefer short-term contracts so they can shop for the best deal. If the franchisor offers you replacement accounts, you may have to pay a new referral or marketing fee.

- **Performance obligations.** You may have to meet minimum monthly performance or growth requirements. If you don't, you may lose the franchise. Worse yet, you may not have the right to a refund of your franchise fee.

- **Payment for services.** The franchisor collects payment from your customers. If the customer doesn't pay, you don't get paid. The franchisor may not be legally obligated to force the customer to pay, but if the franchisor sues for payment, you may have to pay the legal costs.

- **Personal guarantees.** Many franchisors require franchisees to personally guarantee the obligations of the franchise business. This means that if your business assets don't cover your franchise obligations, you could lose personal assets, like your home or car.

- **Anti-competition rules.** You and your immediate family (your spouse and children) may not be allowed to have an ownership interest or perform services in another cleaning business, even if your family members don't have an ownership interest in your janitorial franchise. This restriction may continue even after your franchise ends.

The FTC's Franchise Rule

By law, a franchisor must give you a detailed disclosure document. The disclosure document should include:

- the total number of franchises, and the number of franchises terminated or not renewed during the previous year;

- the bases and assumptions for any claims about potential earnings or the earnings of existing franchisees;

- the cost of starting and maintaining the business;

- the names, addresses and telephone numbers of at least 10 franchisees who live closest to you (names, addresses and telephone numbers of at least 100 franchisees is required in some states, including Maryland) ;

- the background and experience of the franchisor's key executives;

- a fully audited financial statement of the franchisor;

- any lawsuits against the franchisor or its directors by franchisees; and

- The responsibilities you and the franchisor have to each other once you've purchased the franchise.

You should receive the disclosure document at least 10 business days before you pay any money or legally commit yourself to buying a franchise. Ten business days should give you enough time to review the document, get answers to your questions, talk to franchisees and get advice from an attorney, accountant or business advisor.

Protect Yourself

Buying a franchise is a big decision. Before you commit, take the following precautions:

- **Read the company's disclosure document.** Review it carefully to learn more about your obligations, the litigation history of the franchisor and failure rates. This information will help you decide whether franchisees are dissatisfied with the franchise.

- **Talk to other franchisees.** Don't rely only on the information the franchisor gives you. Talk to current and former franchisees about their experiences with the franchisor. Their names, telephone numbers and addresses should be in the company's disclosure document. The franchisor may refer you directly to franchisees that are known to be successful. Don't rely on references the company selects.

- **Contact your state franchise administrator.** If you live in California, Hawaii, Illinois, Indiana, Maryland, Minnesota, New York, North Dakota, Rhode Island, South Dakota or Virginia, your state has an office that regulates the offer and sale of franchises. Contact your state franchise administrator before you invest. Ask if the franchise you're considering is registered to offer franchises in your state. If you live in Maryland, call the Maryland Attorney General's Office at (888) 743-0023, or visit www.oag.state.md.us. If you live outside of Maryland, you can find the name of your state franchise administrator, by calling the North American Securities Administrators Association at (202) 737-0900 or visit www.nasaa.org. You also may contact your state Attorney General (www.naag.org) or Better Business Bureau (www.bbb.org) for more information.

- **Get all promises in writing.** If a salesperson tells you that the franchisor will give you accounts near your home, but the written agreement defines the geographic area more broadly, it's what's in the written agreement that counts. If a provision in the agreement is different from anything you discussed with the salesperson, demand that the written agreement be changed. If a salesperson tells you that you should be able to make $12 to $15 an hour, make sure that prediction is included in the disclosure document. If the salesperson or franchisor won't agree, walk away from the deal.

- **Review the franchise agreement carefully.** It's important to understand all the conditions of the agreement. It controls your relationship with the franchisor. Make sure the agreement spells out the details so there are no surprises.

- **Understand your obligations.** As a franchisee, you may have to pay royalties and other fees. Find out exactly what types of fees you'll have to pay, how much you'll pay and how often.

- **Investigate claims about potential earnings.** The estimated value of the package of accounts you buy may not reflect the income you'll earn from servicing those accounts. Find out how the company assigns a value to the accounts. Ask how many franchisees made the represented income and where those franchisees are located.

- **Be cautious when financing.** While financing your purchase through the franchisor may seem appealing, the terms of the financing agreement may not be the best deal for you. For example, you may have to sign a note to secure the debt and agree to terms that could make it tough for you to sue the company if you wanted to cancel your agreement. Before you agree to franchisor financing, be sure you understand all the terms of the deal.

- **Consider getting professional advice.** Ask a lawyer, accountant or business advisor to review the disclosure document and franchise agreement. The money and time you spend on professional help may save you from a bad investment.

For More Information

The FTC also publishes a series of consumer brochures on franchising and business opportunities. For free copies, contact the Consumer Response Center, Federal Trade Commission, Washington, DC 20580, 1-877-FTC-HELP (1-877-382-4357), TDD: (202) 326-2502, www.ftc.gov.

The State of Maryland also publishes investor brochures about franchises and business opportunities. For copies, or for more information about Maryland's requirements regarding the sale of franchises and business opportunities, contact the Office of the Attorney General, Maryland Securities Division, 200 St. Paul Place, Baltimore, MD 21202, (410) 576-6360, www.oag.state.md.us, email: securities@oag.state.md.us.

Glossary of Terms

Disclosure Document - A written document that outlines the general franchise offering, including background information of the franchisor, a summary of the franchise agreement, and a list of current franchisees.

Franchise Agreement or Franchise Contract - The written document that spells out the legally binding obligations between the franchisor and the franchisee.

Franchise Fee - The purchase price for the franchise.

Franchisee - Any person who buys or invests in a franchise.

Franchisor - Any person who sells a franchise.

Management or Service Fee - A fee paid the franchisee for extra or ongoing support, such as providing additional or substitute accounts.

Royalty Fee - A specific payment made by the franchisee for the right to use the franchisor's trademark. In most instances, the franchisee pays this fee throughout the term of the agreement, regardless of anythIng else the franchisor may or may not do.

The FTC works to prevent fraudulent, deceptive and unfair business practices in the marketplace and to provide information to help consumer's spot stop and avoid them. To file a complaint or get free information on consumer issues, visit ftc.gov or call toll-free, 1-877-FTC-HELP (1-877-382-4357); TTY: 1-866-653-4261. Watch a video, How to File a Complaint, at ftc.gov/video to learn more. The FTC enters consumer complaints into the Consumer Sentinel Network, a secure online database and investigative tool used by hundreds of civil and criminal law enforcement agencies in the U.S. and abroad.

Here are a list of Janitorial Franchises:

Jani-King.com

- Start A Commercial Cleaning Franchise with the King of Clean
- If you're starting a business, who better to partner with than the global leader in the ever-growing $100 billion commercial cleaning industry?
- As a Jani-King franchise owner, you can start a **commercial cleaning franchise** with an investment that works in today's uncertain economy.

System4usa.com

Office Cleaning Business

System4 is the solution for all business commercial cleaning needs. With more than 50 years experience in the commercial cleaning business, we know what works for you. A System4 office cleaning business professional will sit down with you to create a customized work schedule that itemizes each service you want performed. You tell us what you need, when you need it. We deliver.

A System4 office cleaning business provides services that are specific to your facility. The equipment, cleaning products and staff training are customized to meet your facility's requirements. We successfully service customers ranging in size from "big box" retail and multi-tenant offices to small individual businesses. Medical to daycare, factory to showroom, whatever your commercial cleaning needs, a System4 office cleaning business provides a full range of services for any facility:

- Country Club
- Municipal Buildings
- Conference Center
- Restaurant
- Day Care
- Retail - Local and "Big Box"
- Dialysis Center
- Salon
- Fitness Center
- Schools
- Apartment Complex
- Hotel
- Auto Dealership
- Medical Facility
- Bank
- Movie Theater
- Bowling Alley
- Office - General
- Church
- Office - Multi Tenant

Our Business is Cleaning Your Business

Chapter 3: Planning for Future Layoffs
(Get an Education)

Start with a field of study

Go to... http://www.classesusa.com/edu-learn-more/30401-page1.cusa

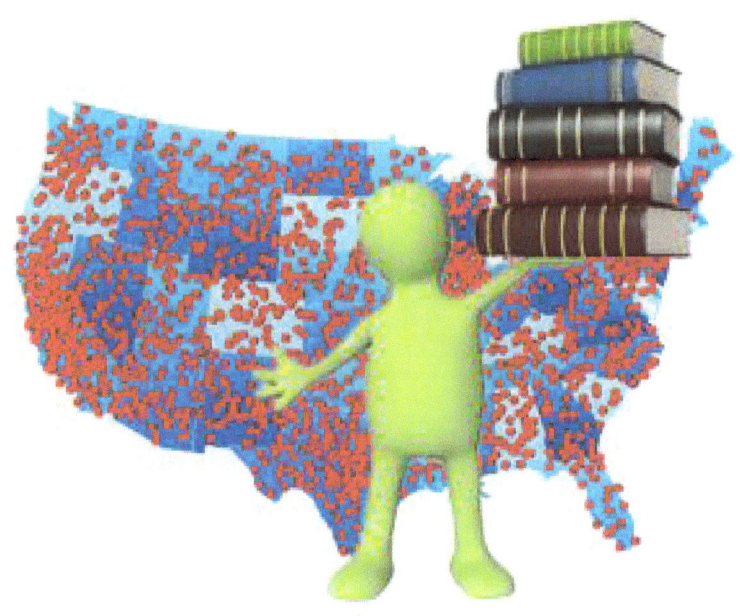

Earn Your Degree On Your Terms Online - Grant Funding May Be Available.

Here are some Questions and Answers from ask.com about free courses on line and how to get them.

Q&A for: Free Online Classes

what websites offer free online classes?

Author: Brandon B

- I would like to find some free online classes to help prepare my recent high-school graduate for college in the fall. What websites offer free online courses, or affordable courses that can help teens prepare for college and are affordable? Can my teenager earn academic credit for those courses?

Answer Question　　　　In Topic: **HIGH SCHOOLS**Tags: **FREE ONLINE CLASSES**

My absolute favorite is Academic Earth.
http://academicearth.org/ it has a wide variety of free lecture series,
and you can take courses for credit for a fee.

Answered by: Robert L.

Where can I find free online vocational classes?

Author: Heather H.

- I'm out of work and trying to fluff up my resume to qualify for a new job.
Are there online sites which can offer free vocational job training?

Answer Question　　　　In Topic: **HIGH SCHOOLS**Tags: **FREE ONLINE CLASSES**

Luckily in this day and age you can find free online classes for just
about anything, including vocational classes. Some URLs include
www.gcflearnfree.org, and www.free-ed.net.

Answered by: Christopher R.

- ### Where can I receive free online classes?

Author: Eric V.

I love to learn but I don't have the money to go back to school. Can you tell me
what online school will allow me to access some of their classes for free?

Answer Question　　　　In Topic: **HIGH SCHOOLS**Tags: **FREE ONLINE CLASSES**

Although getting a degree or certification usually requires payment
for courses there are a few websites, even Universities that offer
free classes online. Check out http://oedb.org/library/beginning-
online-learning/200-free-online-classes-to-learn-anything

Answered by: Jose F.

- ### Are there free online classes to learn CPR?　Author: Nigel N.　My

sister in law had a heart attack and fell. I would like to take a CPR class.
Are there free online classes to learn CPR?

Answer Question

There cannot be online classes to learn CPR.Usually this an hands on training given by the local fire department or EMS people.You can check with your local emergency departments for scheduled classes.   Answered by: Alexander X.

- **Are there any CNA schools online that offer low cost or free classes?**

Author: Kevin R.   I want to be a nurse's assistant, but I'm not sure where to start. I need to find a low cost or free online classe. Are there any CNA schools that are like that?

Answer Question

There are no free programs currenlty avialable for you to obtain a CNA license or diploma from any school. Public schools would be a cheaper option, but none are free.
Answered by: Dylan B.
Learning something new can be a start to a new career or business idea.

Chapter 4: How To Get a Dollar

Purchase my book, **Financial Freedom ONE: Special Guide to Understanding Investing.**

Go to Page 27 to 30

It will show you how to get a dollar.

Go to Page 28 to 29

Learn How to Work hard and study your Customers.

Chapter 5: How to Save a Dollar

Purchase my book, **Financial Freedom ONE: Special Guide to Understanding Investing.**

Go to Pages 31 to 33

Account Setup & Tax Free accounts

Go to Page 92 to 101

Chapter 6: How to Spend a Dollar Wisely

Purchase my book, **Financial Freedom ONE: Special Guide to Understanding Investing**.

Go to Page 31

Chapter 7: Market Trends in a Recession

Purchase my book, **Financial Freedom ONE: Special Guide to Understanding Investing.**

Must read pages 42 to 54 to Understand

How to Read the Financial charts

Then continue below....

[Market Timing Research](#)

How to use Factor Seasonal Charts to Improve Your Trading and Investing

Archive for the 'Stock Charts' tag

[Market Timing Dow Jones Forecasts Using Volume and Monetary Policy](#)

We've just completed a major new study here at Market Timing Research on volume cycles in conjunction with seasonal cycles. Using our same proprietary method for developing price seasonals, we did the same analysis for yearly volume to see if volume does indeed go up as prices go up, and down as prices drop, and to see if it could explain volatility in certain times of the year. Sure enough it does, and when there are periods of disconnect between volumes and price, this may bespeak to an insecure market or periods of volatility that can be used to your benefit. The following charts show what we're talking about.

To our knowledge, no one has ever done this type of analysis previously or produced this type of chart before. As usual, we are market timer firsts. The stock charts suggests we should see a sharp spike UP in the market around now, though that would have to be confirmed with the lunar seasonal.

*Notice that Market Timing depends on the price and season of the stock, meaning is it the right time and industry. It is forecasted and predicted during the trading cycle of a stock.

When to purchase a stock at a low price and when you think it will go high.

Market Timing is a key component in predicting the movement of a stock.

SEE CHART on next page

The other factor seasonal we'd like to highlight is the DJI typical price pattern in years when the government is doing everything possible to provide easy money, as the market has about an 80% correlation with this trend. You can see the forward expectations if this pattern is to hold, once again forecasting a near term bump UP against all expectations.

Naturally you can find lots of individual stocks obeying their seasonal tendencies in our monthly newsletters. Just grab a sample subscription and see for yourself all the money you could be making with this insider information.

Written by Market Timer

May 25th, 2010 at 5:03 pm

Posted in Dow Jones Index

Tagged with dji, djia, market timer, monetary policy, Stock Charts, volume

The S&P 500's Differing Seasonal Trends in Recessions vs. Expansions

The S&P 500 Follows different Seasonal trends during Recessions (RED) than during Expansions (Green)

Examining stock market trends in different fundamental economic, monetary and even political environments reveals a multitude of profitable trading opportunities, as well as easily avoided pitfalls.

Today let's look at the Factor Seasonal Trends for the S&P 500 during recessions compared to expansions.

You can see the S&P 500 trends dramatically different in these two different fundamental environments.

During recessions (shown in RED) the S&P 500 tends to have a brief January rally ending in mid-February. You can see the expected spring rally is flattened out in recessions.

Active traders should expect to see a lot of indicator whipsaws in the traditional spring rally period during recessions as the market trends sideways instead of up.

The S&P then sees a steep decline in late summer through October before a volatile sideways market grays the hairs of investors during the early winter months.

Contrast that to the S&P 500s seasonal trends during business cycle expansions (shown in GREEN).

In expansions January tends to see little upward movement but the Spring Rally strengthens considerably until Mid-July when the index hits a sharp – but short – downtrend. The autumn months remain seasonally weak but those weaknesses shows as flat, sideways trend in expansions rather than the sharp, gut-wrenching downturns in recessions.

Finally the S&P 500 picks up the final two months of the year showing a strong November and December rally.

You can easily see how profitable analyzing the FACTOR seasonal trends — seasonal trends broken down by the differing economic, monetary and political environments – can be. And the Recessions vs. Expansion Factor Seasonal Trend are just one of several we've found has a dramatic impact on market trends.

Written by Market Timer

October 22nd, 2009 at 7:55 pm

Posted in S&P 500

Tagged with S&P 500, Seasonal Trends, Stock Charts

Simplified version:

Three Trends to watch for recovery out of a recession

1). Employment
2). Housing
3). Bank Interest Rates

Employment is the first indicator to watch in 2012.

Jobs created vs. Jobs in the industry

Search 5,277,245 Jobs across the Web

Find Jobs by Category

- Accounting / Finance
- Administrative / Clerical
- Architecture / Engineering
- Art / Graphic Design / Media
- Biotech / Science
- Computer / Technology
- Customer Service
- Executive / Management
- Health Care / Nursing
- Human Resources
- Legal / Paralegal
- Marketing / PR / Advertising
- Restaurant / Hotel
- Retail
- Sales / Business Development
- Software / QA
- Teaching
- Truck Driving
- Transportation / Logistics
- Writing / Freelance
- Part-time / Temporary
- Summer / Seasonal
- Entry Level / Internships

Part-time or Full time

As long as jobs become plentiful in the coming years, the economy will grow. Whether there is an upswing in hiring part-time or full-time workers, this is an important indicator to watch. What are businesses doing to increase money flow in the Stock Market? The more businesses hire people; people in turn can spend money from what they earned into the free market for goods and services. This has become the business cycle of economics.

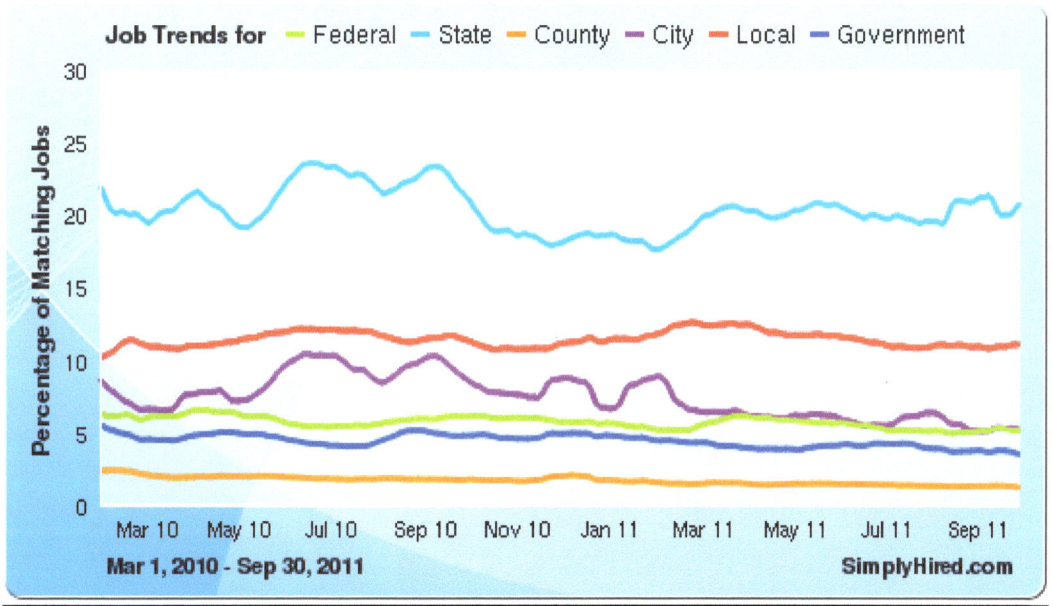

As you can see from the job trend, local cities, County, Federal & government need to create jobs in all sectors. However, the State overall creates more jobs since the population is growing from state to state.

If more money is invested and given to states to build roads, city & state buildings, this will in turn create a vast amount of jobs.

Government money needs to be invested in these sectors in order for the economy to improve.

When you start to see a growth in job creation from a State and local city level, the unemployment rate will decrease and jobs will be plentiful.

HOUSING:

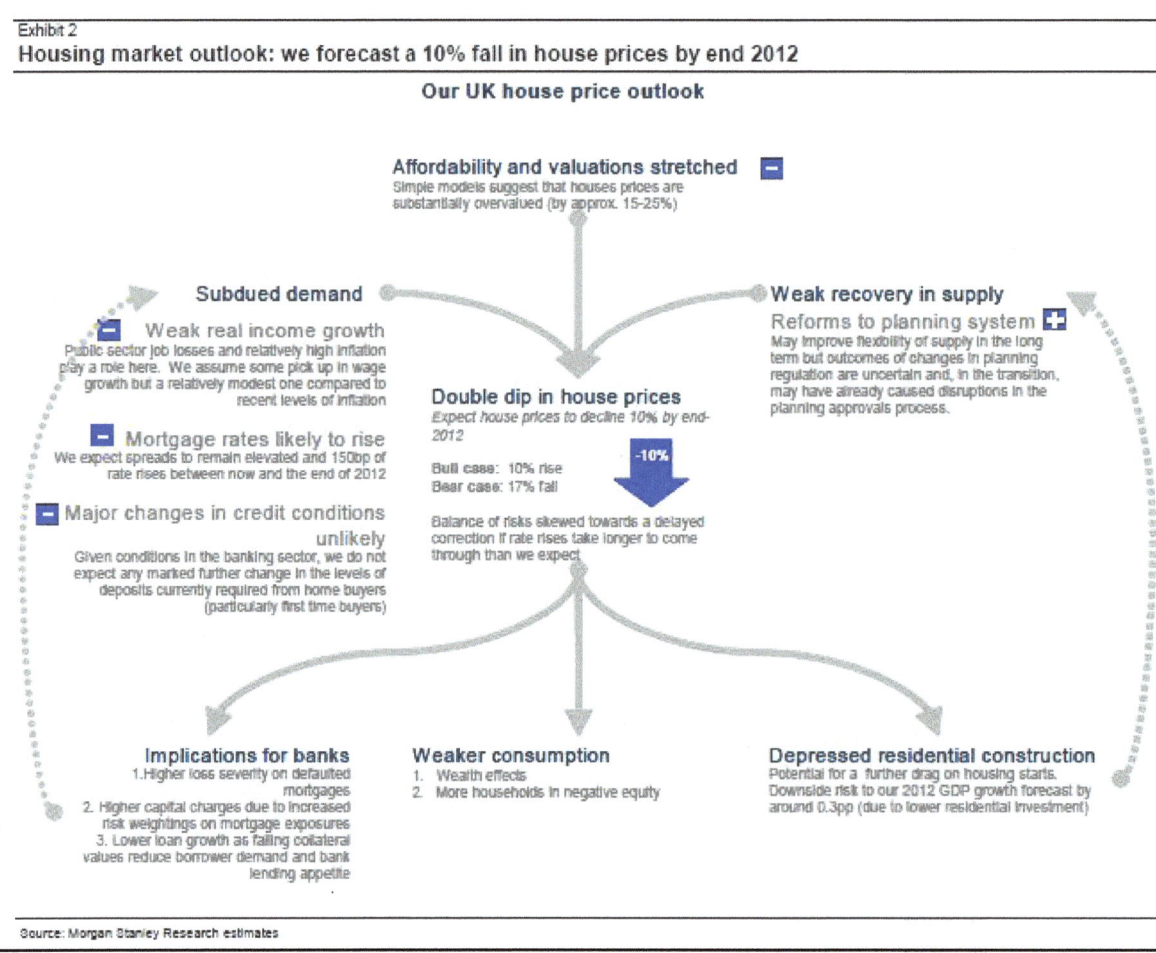

Exhibit 2
Housing market outlook: we forecast a 10% fall in house prices by end 2012

Our UK house price outlook

Source: Morgan Stanley Research estimates

No Demand for new housing is predicted through 2012.
No Financing is given to homeowners from banks to purchase homes.

Banks need to lend to homeowners looking to purchase new housing.

Watch for trends of banks making product packages for 1st time homeowners. Attractive interest rates for first time homeowners are needed by banks to attract new business.

The Trend in the Housing Market

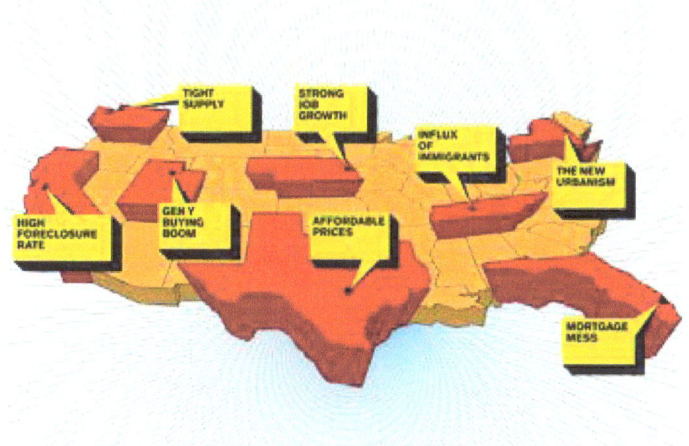

As the housing market improves look for trends in the U.S. economy to improve in parts of the states. **_West Coast_** needs to **stop the foreclosure** rate. **_Mid-Western States_** needs improved **Job growth**. The **_East Coast_** needs **Affordable housing** and handles the **influx of immigration** into urban cities.

West coast has the highest foreclosure rate in the U.S. More Foreclosures are expected through 2012 in the West.

Loans and modifications are not making an impact into the housing market.

Banks need to stop the foreclosures by putting money into the homeowners hand so they can leverage their mortgages. Watch for trends in the west to see if the economy improves. The trend to watch is the lending practices by the banks, modifications increased in the west for improvements.

Bank Interest Rates

Banks lend out money based on the interest rate given to them by the government.

Interest is collected from the money you deposit into your savings or checking account.

Banks invest in bad unsecure investments worldwide which causes Bank failures and massive bailouts from the government. The banking industry as a whole needs to loosen strict policies in regards to their lending practices. Increase loan opportunities to small business and home owners who are in default. If Banks do this they will increase the monetary flow throughout the world and U.S. economy.

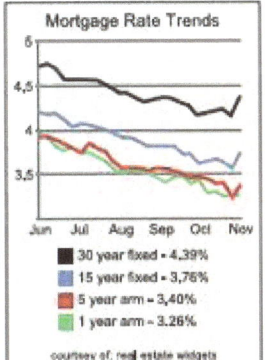 **Mortgage Rate** trends *interest rates* are starting to be lower than expected. As the mortgage rates drop to new lows, Banks will be able to offer more attractive rates for homeowners.

Look for this trend to continue throughout 2012 to present election year.

Notice the **30 year** fixed rate and **15 year** terms are lower than expected.

Chapter 8: How to Invest That Dollar in a Recession

The best way to invest a dollar in a recession is to do cash only business. No more credit cards. Use only cash to do business.

Purchase goods from businesses that are going out of business.

Also Purchase my book **Financial Freedom ONE:
A Special Guide to Understanding Investing**

Read Pages 27 to 31

As per capita, Europeans save more cash than Americans.
The savings per household show that Ireland saves more....

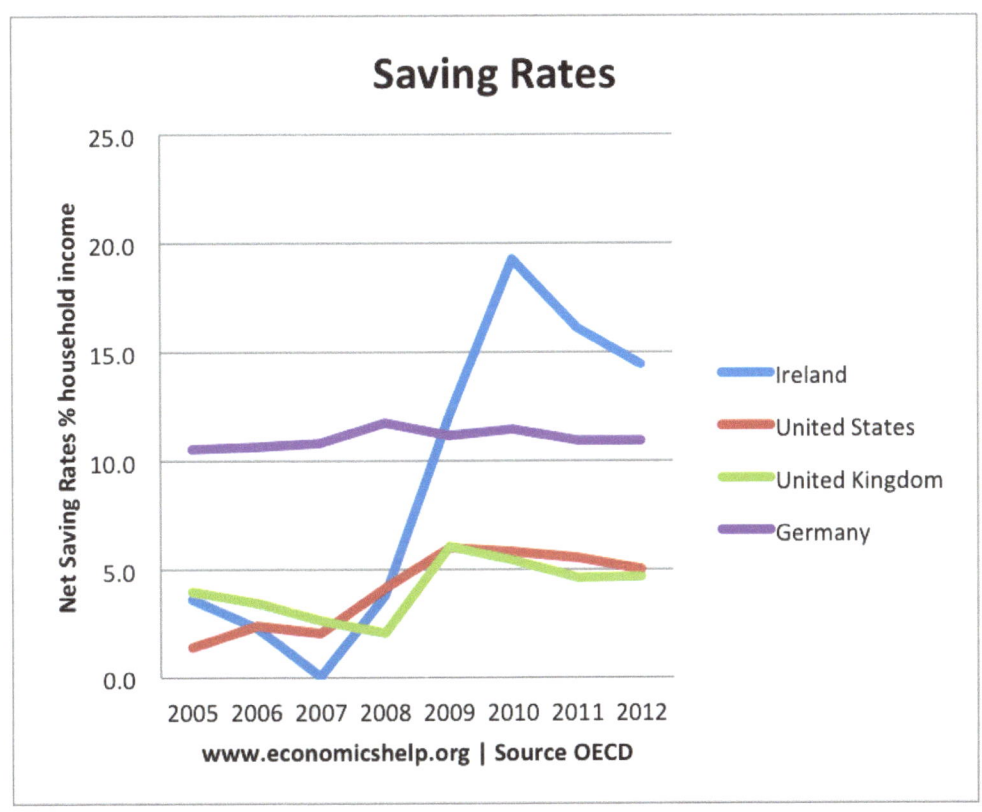

Purchase my book **Financial Freedom ONE:**
A Special Guide to Understanding Investing

Read Page 32 on *How to Save and Where to Save*
Your Money?

Happiness in the United States

Taken all together, how would you say things are these days. Would you say that you are:

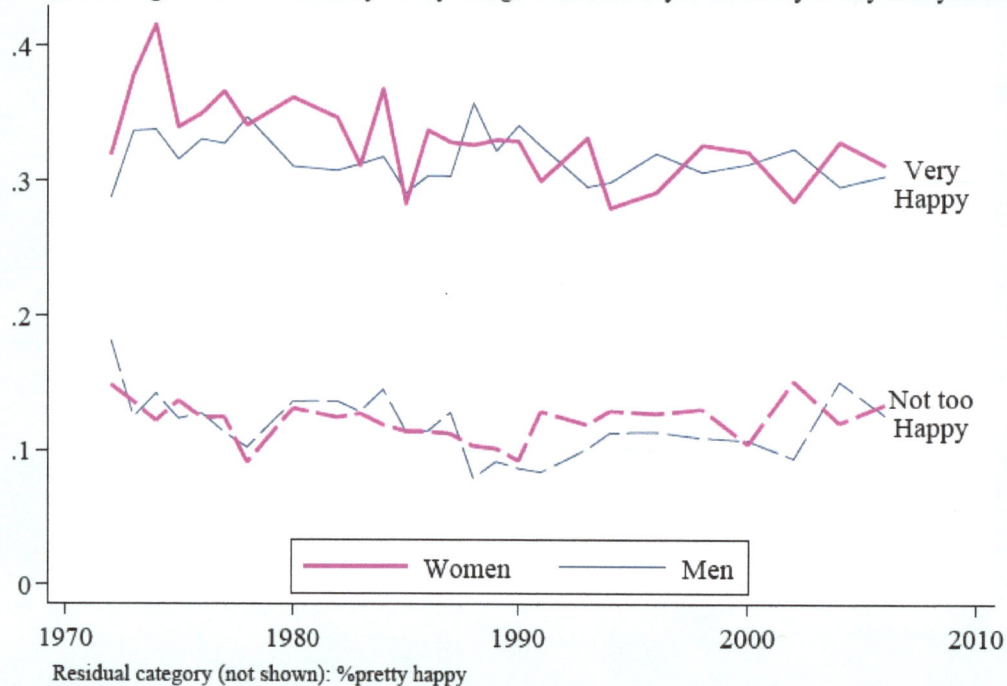

Residual category (not shown): %pretty happy

During the course of 30 years a survey was taken to see if people were happy today financially, emotionally and healthy. As you can see, due to the current economic statistics of Lay-offs, Unemployment, No Opportunity of getting a job within 3 months, Housing Foreclosures and overall political climate, People are not happy. Especially Men overall are not happy with current job situations, housing, health etc.

Only the 1% of the world's richest are happy and do not stress about money, health, housing or political climate.

As indicated in this book, Plan to be happy by working for yourself, building wealth and establishing a strong and recession proof successful business.

Spend your savings wisely on foreclosed property, bargain sales and businesses going out of business. Your money saved will be your "<u>Financial Freedom Too.</u>"